*As I*ₛ

PITT POETRY SERIES

As Is

JULIA SPICHER KASDORF

UNIVERSITY OF
PITTSBURGH PRESS

Published by the University of Pittsburgh Press, Pittsburgh, Pa., 15260
Manufactured in the United States of America
Printed on acid-free paper
10 9 8 7 6 5 4 3 2 1

ISBN 13: 978-0-8229-6702-6
ISBN 10: 0-8229-6702-2

Cover art: Helen O'Leary from *Home Is a Foreign Country* (2018). Courtesy of the artist.
Cover design: Alex Wolfe

For Philip

CONTENTS

As I₅

To fix it is to put an end to it. Let me show it to you unfixed.

—Wallace Stevens, *The Necessary Angel*

They Call It a Strip Job

Stretch of 219—old road out of West Virginia
they still call the Mason-Dixon Highway—

widens and divides at the Meyersdale bypass,
the right lane closed, drowned by a mound

of inside-out hillside, so I drift to the left, now
running both ways, as the scent of mud floods

in through the vents. All my growing up among
men who skinned hills to scrape their seams,

I've never seen a strip job this deep or trucks this big.
No one works the job tonight, which stays light

long after moonrise, no one hears me cuss.
Remember Strypeeze, the goop Mom painted onto

antiques, how it burned your skin and buckled varnish?
Ever feel how hot wax, stroked on the bone beneath

your brow, stings with the flick of a stylist's wrist?
Ms. Woitek, turquoise eyelids and coral lips, danced

on stage at the Silver Dollar out on Route 30,
everyone said, but who had seen? Her specialty:

one semester of creative writing for eleventh graders.
She's gone by now. O, let her rest on a green hill

somewhere. Let the light hold until I make it home
from a job where I sat in a clean, quiet room

in a brick hall built during the century that built
railroads to haul coal from these hills and logs

from those mountains to prop open deep mines
or to make the ties that held the rails that became

ways to walk out of those towns. O, how did I come
to get paid to sit in a clean, quiet room and listen

to lines written by coal miners' grandchildren, listen
until we find the spots that smolder or sing.

Sweetgum

Drag scrap lumber and pre-war dresser
drawers from the sidewalk to the cellar
then let them rest awhile in the dark.

Like the wren who doesn't mind repetition
or euphony, keep pulling twigs and feathers
from the bird box. Let go your desire to wrap

it up; closure's a hoax. Like grief, this labor
requires long walks, bicycle rides, and talking
out loud when no one else is around.

Use the same words the newspaper uses, yet not.
Offer student work, botched. *Never mention
poetry in a poem*. Try to render the redbud's

shaggy, plum branches and scraps of cloud stuck
in the runs between ridges above town. *Each poem
is about what it's about, and also about verse.*

Pre-war refers to the Second World War—so
the gal can also whip up a pie crust in a jiffy! *Don't
mention politics in a poem* Galway said sadly,

I see only one beautiful phrase in this whole piece.
See how the sweetgum tree dangles balls
studded with shrieking sparrow beaks:

cukoo-birs, bommy knockers, bir balls, gum balls.
In 1615, herbalist Francisco Hernandez mixed
sweetgum with tobacco to dissipate foul humors.

Yehuda said, *The poem is a vaccine you brew*
in your own body from myriad diseases, meaning
make use of whatever's at hand, my friend.

Testing

Testing? What testing! I soak dried beans,
revving up my sewing machine. We self-isolate,
we wave at our neighbors, concoct *quarantinis*,
listen to *quarantunes*, queue the *quaranTV*, sleep

more than we have in a long time. My labors
deemed non-essential, I clean the freezer
and cupboards as if dusting the last crumb
from under the Angel of Death. I weed

my closet of business attire I no longer need.
Passover, Holy Week, Week of the Pink Moon,
worst week until the next week comes. We lose
two thousand a day, not counting thousands

not counted. We lose thousands of jobs.
Let not your hearts be troubled. Priests celebrate
Easter in empty churches, reminding us hope arose
in grief, under military occupation: *Woman behold*

your son, son behold your mother. In Boro Park,
men bob in prayer on the sidewalk, Torah scrolls
out in the sun as if they were still in the wilderness.
No harm will befall you. Nor will plague fall

upon your tent. We trace contacts, crave beauty
and touch, reading novels on screens. I see
how invisibly some people die. I search for yeast
and seeds grown as scarce as tissue and soap.

With an abundance of caution, I leave a vase
of tulips and a handwritten note on a shelf
by the door of the retirement home. Onion snow
falls on our daffodils and coral quince blossoms.

Fourteen days on a ventilator, texts came, fifteen
mornings I lit a ruby cup and let the flame draw
oxygen from the living room until it was finished.
Hope is a thing with feathers. Hope is a thing

that breathes. *One cannot truly know hope,* Merton
wrote, *unless he has found how like despair
hope can be.* At dinner, we fell silent watching
a woman at the Little Free Library on our street.

She opened a book to read the flap, turned it to read
the back, then slowly returned it to choose another,
street light flickering on over her head. She looked
and looked until she finally left, taking nothing.

City of the Dead

With each report from Italy, I see Orvieto
empty, those afternoons after *pranzo*
I walked cobblestones in October sun alone

with the child. Wasps hummed on split figs.
The tourist shop by the *Duomo* stayed open,
but how often could we visit those shelves

of wooden Pinocchios? And the *Duomo*,
golden crust on blood-stained altar
clothes, frescoed devils flapping above

the Last Judgment. Like feral cats
fed on the doorsteps by *matrona*
in black dresses, we roamed aimlessly

every day the same until we kicked
windfall chestnuts over sloping cobbles
all the way down to that other city

where Etruscan glyphs mark stone lintels,
grass paves the streets, and a coiled black
snake suddenly woke to my scream.

War

The visiting poet spoke in intonations that come
from no place, peering over half-glasses,

Queen Dido—you recall her from a high school
Latin class or maybe a Great Books course? No

flicker on the faces beneath ball caps
and bar tour hair-dos, kids who come to college

because they need decent jobs. *Um, then*
the poet stammered. Listening in the front row:

blanched local beauty with a wasp's waist
and dark eyes who wrote about farm implements

rusting in morning fog, an opossum stunned
in the lane. She'd rushed to my office that day

to apologize for coming late to class—it's that
she'd left her husband again, clothes in a trash bag.

She regretted the expensive textbooks stranded
in his truck, just too many guns on the farm

to go back. Brain-injured in Iraq, he patrolled
hedge rows with a rifle until she hid his boots

according to one poem. In another, she woke
to him clutching her throat. In Dido's Temple,

the frieze of Troy displayed the carnage, so
Aeneas could finally speak of the battle. No

wonder the Queen fell so hard for him before
he left Carthage, her body aflame in his wake.

What the Hemlock Said

Think of the energy it took
four brothers and their mules

to hack through roots, pry rocks,
haul earth, dig the race to divert

enough stream to turn a wheel.
Think of the wheel splashing

power to push blades the length
of their neighbors' logs. Think of

tree limbs smoldering under mud
and leaves to bake charcoal to fuel

the stone furnaces at Monroe
and Greenwood to smelt the ore

dug up from the earth around here
to forge implements of civil war.

Climate Change with Daughter and Tomatoes

That wet August, leaves grew spotted then dried
and the tomatoes refused to ripen, so I bought

two bushels at a farm stand, washed jars, gathered
the brass rings I once slid onto my arms like slaves

in a Bible story illustration of the way God plagued
Pharaoh until Moses split the sea and they walked free.

One pot to scald skins, one to seal the lids. I dipped
tomatoes into steam while my daughter cored

and peeled at the table. We packed jars, spooned salt,
screwed the rings over flats, racks of seven jars each

boiled in their baths late into the night until 48 quarts
cooled on towels, each *ping* pronouncing a seal.

The next morning, our winter's hoard gleamed
on dim cellar shelves. I have always believed things

will turn out with work and hope, maybe not quite
what you thought, but somehow, yet when I opened

one of those quarts, it reeked of rot. Nothing for it
but to haul it all up the hill in a wagon, dump jar after

jar until the compost looked like a heap of red organs
that later grew a coat of soft, white mold.

Gideons

On clear September mornings, men in neckties
and gold-buttoned, blazers with Palestinian lamps
on their lapel pins appear on campus, cardboard cartons
on the walk beside dress shoes; tiny, green Testaments

in hand. From a distance, I spy them and turn, unable to take,
unable to refuse, unable to make conversation with men
who seem to have stepped from the '70s when my dad
belonged to the Christian businessmen's organization

named for the prophet who, with his band of 300 men
and torches, horns, and clay jars defeated the Midianites,
as thick as locusts, their camels without number, later
called Bedouins and founding members of OPEC.

The Midianites trampled fields planted by Israelite settlers
delivered out of the house of slavery in Egypt. History
on repeat, I can't stop seeing bodies in streets, arms raised,
citizen's bodies beaten with night sticks, pepper-sprayed,

eyes cleansed with milk. The connection to Gideon?
A band of brave ones, noise, smashing of jars, *A sword
for the Lord and for Gideon!* The prophet demolished
Baal's altar and called Israel back to their true God,

all they needed for a king. Then the story takes a turn best left
in the Bible: Gideon's seventy sons from plundered wives,
a Shechemite concubine bore Abimelech whose name
means *my father is king*. The 45th president—with lips like

Mussolini who lied, *The truth is that men are tired of liberty*—
set the National Guards on his own citizens. Not the first time,
and when has this nation changed without fire and guns?
Gideon's men presented the heads of two Midianite captains:

What have we done in comparison to all you have done to us?
Blasting a path through bodies with tear gas, the 45th president
posed with a Bible in front of a boarded-up church. *He did not
pray. He did not mention George Floyd, he did not mention*

the agony of people subjected . . . the bishop charged from afar.
On Sunday afternoons back in the '70s, my Dad filled the car
with cartons of Bibles covered to complement motel decor:
bittersweet orange, woodgrain, ecru lace, federal blue, avocado,

and we'd drive the Lincoln Highway or Route 70, stopping
at spiked sputnik signs and parking lots beside slag heaps
or fallow fields. I'd wait in the car while he met the manager.
Success was his smile striding back to fetch a box of Bibles

to place on bedside stands, less if the Testaments were shut up
in drawers with the phone book. Maybe a weary traveler
would find comfort in psalms of praise or lamentation,
guidance in the cryptic words of Jesus: *I did not come*

to bring peace, but a sword. . . . Blessed are the peacemakers.
He never wondered aloud what transpired in those rooms,
what kinds of strangers steal Bibles. His faith in words
on the page certain we'd done enough, leaving books behind.

American Bittersweet

In the bramble between Possum Hollow and Beaver Road,
between my thirty-years-ago school bus route and PA 136:
a torn mattress heaved into the ravine, diapers, soup cans.

At the sight of burnt-orange berries in the tree limbs,
I pull over, pull a knife from the glove box, walk
a gravel access road past *No Trespassing, Columbia Gas,*

brine tanks, petroleum pipes, *Dominion Transmission,*
pull vines from branches while compression sheds hum
upwind from the trailer park where poor kids boarded

the bus. Come fall, Mom would stop the car anywhere
to tear bittersweet from trees and fence rows, then arrange it
on the mantle. She'd swath candles and crèche in crow's foot.

Whatever beauty we found in the woods or roadside, we took
like the shotgun shells we shoved onto our finger tips,
red and green plastic shafts with clackety brass caps.

When a white pick-up drives by, I stride to my car, casual.
Somewhere, someone spotted me on a monitor. I pull off
before the truck turns around, but he follows me out

onto Edna Road, past rows of company homes beneath
the boney dump from Edna No. 1 and Edna No. 2 mines.
Here, the bus picked up a Black boy who lettered in wrestling.

We never called Edna a patch town. We didn't know
that term, or that Black sharecroppers, driven north
by the boll weevil, took jobs in the mines

and helped break the strikes. Growing up, taking
whatever we could from that place, we didn't recognize
history or anything out of the ordinary.

At Cross Creek Park

All day on highways, I arrived at a shaded lane
that concludes in a parking lot with a restroom

like a fairytale cottage: stone veneer below
chocolate siding. A white-haired guard

in uniform leaned against his spotless, white truck.
What a gorgeous day for December, I began.

Yeah, but next week will be twelve degrees.
I told him I grew up nearby but moved away,

and the place sure has changed in recent years.
So many trucks on the roads today, and where

do they take all that flow-back? *Ohio, on 70
mostly*, he replied. *But it's been quiet here*

*except last week when they put in that privy.
Came all the way from Texas. A big crane*

just dropped it on the hole, one and done!
I didn't ask what lay behind his booth or why

a county park needs a guard with a gun.
When we ran out of phrases to exchange,

I drove away. Seven well pads, spilled waste,
dead fish, old-growth trees cut by mistake

I later learned online. The restroom shows up
in a piece that promises millions to townships

that lease to drillers. But that day, oblivious,
the sun just shone on both of us as hunters

in blaze orange vests vanished into the woods.

Eastern Box Turtle

This pair of eyes so much smaller
than mine, yet we both halt: red eyes

—a male—horned beak, clawed feet,
tail, and those glorious golden glyphs

on his perfectly fitted carapace. Mister,
you bring to mind Thomas E. Peachey,

born 1914, my grandpa who tiled a V
beneath the dome of his silo for grandma

Vesta, and when she died, he married
Verna. He farmed until he retired

to work at the planing mill, and all his life
hunted deer on these mountains and carved

his initials and date onto turtle shells.
Once in the last century as I watched

him incise a scuffed plastron
with a pen knife, a trace of blood rose

in one of his letters. Creature,
with apologies for him and his kind,

I turn you over to find no human lines.

American Chestnut Plantation

Utter the phrase and castanets clatter:
nineteenth-century cabins—
especially the bottom logs prone to rot—
floor boards, fence posts, railroad ties,
plantation, plantation, plantation.

    Under the spreading chestnut tree . . .

A third to half of the trees in these woods
were giant chestnuts back then. Autumns,
whatever nuts the squirrels didn't hoard,
hogs and cows foraged to fatten for winter
or holiday's slaughter. Chestnuts
stuffed the turkey, thickened the pudding.

    . . . roasting on an open fire.

Charcoal-scorched chestnut hulls
infuse the streets of New York.

Smelling of human semen,
pale tendrils dangle from trees
in this field, and saplings
flourish in dated, plastic tubes.

    Pull my chestnut out of the fire.

Roots of blighted chestnuts
survive underground and send up
shoots that sprout and wither.

Oh, that old chestnut!

Science will find a Chinese hybrid
and we're left to settle memory's debts.

As Is

Shabbat Shalom I yell, passing Ben's office, because
it's a Friday afternoon in February, and we're all starved
for sunshine. He laughs because he's secular or doesn't expect
that from me, whom he regards as Mennonite, I guess.

He runs Jewish Studies, no simple task, given Palestine.
Once he came for dinner and loved the salad dressing so much,
he asked for the recipe. *What, that? But it's so Dutchy*, I said,
meaning Pennsylvania Dutch, direct from my aunt on a farm,

almost equal parts sugar and vinegar. Our tastes track back
to similar haunts. I sent for a DNA test, and let's just say
there were no surprises, not one drop of Lenape blood,
though there might have been, given Ulrich Speicher's warrant

from Penn's wicked sons. (Was it just a few valleys with cows
over there to one valley with cows over here?) My kid's DNA
tells another tale: English Quakers, Dutch Mennonites, Jews
settled in Ukraine. Her Oma speaks of a black dress passed

to a woman during the terror times, tailored, puffed sleeves,
tiny jet beads sewn at the neck, exquisite except for a stain
and bullet hole in the bodice. Pulled from a Jewish body,
the dress survives, troubling our minds. This week I read a book

about gun violence with students who either loved or resisted
it: *this poet writes by the sentence, not the line*, they claimed.
She doesn't end lines, she breaks them. Near campus, in a bar
across the street from a Mennonite meetinghouse, a boy, back

from three years active duty, got rough with his girl, so strangers—
father and son—tried to stop it. The boy pulled out a gun,
shot them both, wounded the girl, then killed someone else,
plus himself. The strangers were in town for a horse auction.

In Ohio, their funeral drew more than two thousand, many Amish,
and someone recalled that once Dean Beachy could not hawk
a horse, so he said, *Let's just sell it as is; that's how I got my wife
and it worked out alright.* As is. The list of camps the poet's

grandparents survived brings to mind killing fields in Poland
near Mennonite homes where, even hungry after the war,
farmers didn't plow, so grass returned. When West Nickel
Mines Amish School was razed and planted in perennial

pasture before sunrise, leaving nothing to photograph
so the reporters finally went home, a local rabbi said
if they had been Jews, a memorial would have gone up.
They would not forget. Five slain girls, not six million,

nor unknown millions starved, shot, sent to the gulag.
Commissar of Munitions, Stalin said of the Ukrainian famine,
If one man starves it's a tragedy, if millions, it's only statistics.
I cannot get over the sight of the poet's mom, born in a DP camp

in Stuttgart, held high above her own mother's head, red hair
blazing like a torch to show Eleanor Roosevelt the next new
citizen bound for New York. Today, the 45th president declared
a national emergency to erect a wall against immigrants.

Towns in medieval Europe closed their gates because strangers
carried plague, but I grew up during Vietnam with a dream
of Shalom. In the City of Brotherly Love, Ulrich Speicher worked
off his passage before acquiring land at Tulpehocken.

On the *Charming Nancy's* ship list, his name is spelled
Ulrigh Spigher among several other Amish names,
all marked by an illiterate X. Ben Franklin hated those
"swarthy masses" at Germantown, planned English-only

schools. Historians think the *Charming Nancy* belonged
to Benedict Arnold. I, too, write by the sentence,
compose as is, then break my lines.

One must make shift with things as they are.

—Aldo Leopold, *A Sand County Almanac*

Precious Memories Help Yourself

Dad scrawled in marker on a cardboard box
of photographs he set out for all of us, home
to pack up and downsize and resist their pleas

to take the fine china and furniture they'd spent
their lives acquiring. My brothers and me, kids
in the round-cornered snapshot: moppy hair,

Converse before they turned retro, horn-rimmed
aviators before Biden revived them, tenderly
drooping off one brother's shoulder, a shirt

some call "wife beater" or "Dago tee," epithet
children in our grade school called themselves.
In a homemade orange jumper, I pet

cousin Renee's rabbit posed by the carport
in a '70 haze. Next, crisp gray and cream 8 x 10
of the homeplace, circa 1909: milk delivery sleigh

hitched to black horses, three sisters in long skirts
and aprons lined up in the slush, great-grandma Cora
among them, plus the two brothers in Derby hats

who moved to Oregon and Dakota following
Indian Removal. *Help yourself* means take, also
save yourself if you can. Cora Mae's daughter,

Vesta Mae, whose middle name came to me,
stands framed in a shiny black and white
rectangle from the '30s, hair parted down

the middle, eyes closed, the mountain
a gray horizon line high above her head.

Hand Me Down

Who knew that sleepers and black Mary Janes
could gather such freight—robin's egg wool frock
from her godmom, gauze Easter smock worn once,
cheap purple velvet with platter lace collar
the child demanded each Sunday one winter.

She had no patience for trying things on,
so I stretched legs and sleeves against whatever
seemed to fit that week—flat shape on the bed
like a chalk outline—then sorted between
charity, friends, one keepsake. My back ached,
deliberating over those piles until
I'd stand, suddenly dizzy. What's too stained
to save was never the question, instead
I wondered what I could choose to pass on.

Flags

Before anyone told me Persephone's story
I endured it afternoons walking home

from the bus. He'd beckon from beyond
a long rectangle of green blades,

pointed buds, bearded iris blossoms—
lavender, yellow, white, indigo—flags

he called them, for the war dead, then led
me down cellar steps into winter light

under fluorescent tubes. Look: irises bloom
in our June garden, daughter, see whiskered

stripes on tongues that tremble from
the mouths of beasts. How your beauty

opening, opening worries me. Inside
the iris blossom, a part they call an arm

looks like cartilage in a chicken breast,
quivering. Darling, breathe the petals

glistening scent, but promise me
you'll come to no harm.

When I Say *Is That What You're Wearing?*

I mean with the sleeves
of his pullover fleece
                    hanging down to her hands,
                    how can she eat or text
or take a German test?
It drapes over black tights,
                    no visible panty lines,
                    which a mother should
never notice or say.
This is now style, I know,
                    cardigans called *boyfriend*
                    sweaters, as if a garment
could substitute for
his arms around her.
                    But she swims in it,
                    as they say, so huge
it makes her look small.
When I say *Is that*
                    what you're wearing,
                    I mean I'm afraid
that some stranger gazing
on her buns will gobble
                    them in one gulp.
                    She says things won't change
unless we do. True,
but must it be you?

When I Say *Make a List*

I mean I have grown so
weary of her litany
                    of deadlines and duties:
                    homework and tests,
meetings, needy friends,
neglected beloveds;
                    I've seen the minute
                    penciled script littering
the room, plus day planner,
phone calendar. She knows
                    how to manage her time,
                    divide tasks and work
her way down the line
as well as any of us,
                    it's not really that;
                    she just needs to scream
at someone. My mom
would never have stood for it.
                    How else did I become
                    a woman who writes
but can't utter half
of her thoughts out loud?
                    Listen always starts
                    with a list, see?
Write it down so you
can hear yourself think
                    then get to work, quiet-
                    ly crossing things off.

When I Say *Clean Your Room*

I hear the sneeze, see
the swirl of pillows,

            sheets, waded tissues,
            lint, dust, cat dander

clumped under the bed.
I smell incense, smoke

            blown out the window,
            black ash gathering

on the sill. I see clothes
she won't ever wear

            or hang up, yet can't bear
            to pass on. A cactus

and succulents plead
from parched pots

            when I stand at her door,
            eyes darting from mess

to mess, which drives her mad.
Ordering clutter's my drug;

            I can't think one clear thought
            if my desk is a wreck.

When airplanes used to split
her ears, and she wailed,

            I'd uncover a breast
            and soothe her to sleep,

but now all I can do
is say *clean your room*.

When I Say *Okay Take My Car*

I mean I'll take the bus,
fueled by compressed
                 natural gas, low emissions,
                 but fracked with diesel
machines and toxic compounds
hauled in big trucks. I know
                 she'll come home happy
                 with a glowing fuel light,
fenders crusted with
the grey dust that billows
                 off narrow, dirt roads
                 on these ridges. O,
at her age, I drove
highways at ninety
                 in a Plymouth Fury
                 that got fifteen miles
to the gallon, gay '80s,
when Ronald Reagan
                 tore the solar panels
                 off the White House roof
like some teenage brain
unable to see
                 past immediate thrills
                 to whatever disaster
has to come next.
I mean until I hear
                 my Subaru grind up
                 the drive, I won't sleep.

When I Say *It's Your Life*

I mean I'll probably miss
scalding her thermos
              while I brew our coffee
              and scoop the cat litter.
School serves a hot lunch
but I just want to do
              something. It's too late to say
              Get more sleep! Exercise!
Eat something green!
Not long ago it all
              fell to me, holding her
              on my lap at Public Health
when our cheap insurance
wouldn't cover vaccines.
              One doctor, suspecting
              neglect, addressed her:
How many people
sleep in your house,
              how many pets?
              I know she belongs
to herself and a future
I won't live to see.
              I just mean you're enough,
              don't give up or get stuck,
but I hold my tongue
and warm up the soup.

Waking Up with Jerry Sandusky

He snores beside me naked, so I play
possum, tell myself he raped boys

from over the mountain in gym showers
I'll never use, that a person is innocent

as long as he sleeps. Then he shifts, sighs.
I feel the pulse in his pelvis beside

my pelvis. When he stands up, his thighs
seem in great shape for a man his age.

It's a dream, oldest trick in the book,
yet I lie in the dark telling myself

Sandusky is a town in Ohio named
for a Polish fur trader or else

the Wyandot word for *here is pure water.*
Sandusky is a town in Ohio known

for roller coasters and a killer whale
trained to jump for dead fish. Sandusky

is a football field next to Brownson House
in little Washington where Jerry grew up

in a flat above the rec center, and also
Jerry's dad, Art, the athletic director.

Sandusky's in solitary in Greene County,
23 hours a day, three showers a week.

Sandusky is the Germanized spelling
of Sandowski, Sedowski, names lugged into

mills by men who worked 16-hour days then
built homes, a Polish social club, a church

up the hill. Don't let me get sentimental
about the workers and go soft on Sandusky

whose dull face in the newspaper the day
of his arrest made me think of a mill hunk

who hasn't yet learned enough words to speak
in the blast furnace of his new language.

Second Space

To the young editors who *regularize* my texts,
let me say sorry, but back when I learned to type

on machines, not keyboards, it was two strokes
after a period. In that beige room of metal desks,

one semester down the hall from where I hit a wall
each trigonometry test and had to request a hall pass

to go puke in the Girls Room, typing tests were timed:
seven minutes of furious clatter, then we'd pull pulpy

practice sheets from the carriage and circle mistakes,
calibrating our scores from time, word count, errors.

No mysteries and, unlike trig, a skill I could brush up
and use to put a husband through art school. To even

get an interview, you needed 70 words per minute.
Two years later, a Wang blinked luminous, green fonts

on a convex, black screen at my desk. A printer
the size of a VW bug purred in the hall.

Is that when striking the second space became archaic—
like saying *pocketbook* for purse, a place we hid

tampons and other secrets? Once a man called up
my office just as I was about to head out for lunch

offering fifty-dollars in Duane Read cosmetics
if I'd take a survey on pantyhose and disposable

razors. *Hang on, just a few more questions*, he pressed
when I paused. *If you shave your armpits and legs,*

his bland voice snapped to a snarl, *why not clean up
your cunt?* I flung the receiver at my desk set,

trembling, shamed I'd been lured down the shaft
of that mind. Now, we'd say *violation*, but then

I just stared out my fourth-floor window that faced
a wall of windows and imagined that voice in one

of those rectangles, beating off. No one
to tell, no one to blame but myself, I pulled the blind

and tucked that mistake away, like all the rest.

Bruder

If asked to draft the obituary, I'd say he was stout
and chuckled. On a marble mantle in his room
where we lived at Menno House on East 19th,
he lined bargain jars of herring in sour cream,
slivers of scales like the tulle cap his sister wore
when she drove a pick-up with a cap to Manhattan,
swerved through snarls at the end of Canal
onto the bridge, so we could all stride in the gold
light and wind on the boardwalk at Brighton.
       Oh beautiful star the hope of light
       Guiding the pilgrims through the night
Young man toting an old man's valise
to Deutsches House on Washington Mews,
one summer he worked with Amish women
back home to learn to speak Dutch, his hair
and beard bound in a net, plucking guts, stuffing
giblets and necks into carcasses, fingers numb
as stones. Those days, New York felt more dangerous,
and everyone seemed more free. The Strand, filthy
fire trap with spray-painted signs and buried treasure,
Weatherly in the stacks, my purse snatched
from the Bargain Books table. What do you gain
when you lose a brother, a place, a time? First
office job, phone call from across campus:
We have facts for you from Mervin Horst
at Deutsches Bank. Across Greene, up an elevator,
the one fax machine: fuzzy sheet *Hey, look at this!*

Give me a call when you receive! his scrawl
before e-mail, before internet or 9/11,
before desktop printers, bike messengers
jumped green lights in Midtown, smoked
weed on the street to soothe their jitters.
           Shining far through shadows dimmed
           Giving the life for those who long have gone
What words did he learn in Lancaster that summer
gossiping in Dutch, what ardor? Editions of *Martyrs*
Mirror stacked up in his Washington Heights flat,
old suits, sweet tooth, sugar in the blood,
love and judgement, white gospel in the blood
           Shine upon us until the glory dawns.

Short Story

That summer you suffered a crush on X writing
in a room on the other side of your cabin.

You had a husband you called from pay phones,
you also called X, and when his wife picked up,

you hung up on her hello, which you now hope
was a machine. This was before everyone ran

discrete lives on wireless cells. This was when you
believed art required romance and pain, mainly

the tiny disasters you stirred up yourself. You
didn't know what you wanted or what Exxon knew

and had already denied, let alone how lucky you
were. You asked X to drive you in his Corvette

on mountain roads, then told him thanks but that
was about the car. After, no matter how early you

got up, he'd be out at the end of the dock:
legs crossed, bucket hat pulled over his slouch.

I'm just falling, he announced at dinner, *falling
until I hit something*. Finally, you sat down in the sun

and wrote fourteen lines about the end of summer.
Your husband arrived to drive you home. How

little you knew, how hard you'd have to fall.

Valentine with Domestic Life

O, let our hearts flap again, frantic
as the starling trapped in the attic

while snow piled up to Francis's chest
in the garden, crusted and shone. Sparrows

flitted and pecked at a Bradford pear split
by wind, limbs lost to ice. For warmth, we

leaned toward our daughter. *Don't watch me,*
she shouted and waved us away. *Rocket!*

Rocket! she pointed at icicles gleaming
under the eaves. Don't forget her delight

when you beat them with a spade, roots
that might rip the gutters from our roof.

Adrift

He says the house we used
to share's a ship these days
                adrift without me
                there to make him eat
or sleep, meaning time
begins to lose its shape
                without a wife around.
                Once a week he speaks
with check-out clerks
or baggers at the store—
                Hello. Good day.
                I think I have some change—
or phones the friends
who entertain him more
                than I could after all
                those years. It's strange
the scripts we write,
the way routines create
                good forms as surely
                as they dull the heart:
we drift through days
until we finally wake
                to ache alone, together
                or apart. At least
he gets the house.
My rented rooms
                float near and far away,
                baffled as a raft.

Lake Trail, January

On this warm day, it's easy enough to jump
to metaphors: the lichen-crusted tree trunk,

a wild turkey breast ruffed with fine stripes
of tan and brown, or the sap-tipped cones

fallen from a white pine, shadow and light.
Easy to pick up a fat acorn and call its cap

tweed. Or the bleached grass beneath
the powerline, a woman's blond hair

wrecked by the weather. Leaves,
frozen and thawed into brittle slips, stick

to the path which, clotted with ice, runs
like a stream this afternoon. Easy to see

patches of fern moss as scraps of jungle,
mood moss, the shaved scalps of soldiers.

The lake, solid aqua, cross-hatched, mottled,
softens in sun as run-off shimmers down

the spillway in white-rimmed scallops.
Easy to think of time's thin rings hidden

beneath pine bark. Hard to see it all and not
make up names for things. Harder to release

the layers of bright and dull weight we carry
walking this ring of earth around a lake.

Dialogue with Lake Perez

Engineered rain basin,
    sky shine,
        wind bedazzle,

what swims beneath your glitter?

    minnows, fin fish, crayfish

Beneath them?

    tree stumps, mud

Before them?

    forest

Before that?

    a barley field

And before?

    wood hicks, charcoalers, soot

Before?

    tannin staining the stream

Before that?

I can't remember.

And what comes after now?

Hush.

No, what?

Remove your shoes, step in.

We are communal histories, communal books. We are not owned or monogamous in our taste or experience. All I desired was to walk upon such an earth that had no maps.

       —Michael Ondaatje, *The English Patient*

Lit

like tiny leaves of the aspen poplar—

transparent green peridot on my finger

raising your arm's fine hairs like flames

that might blow too close to the creek

or fires that leap over water like glints

the sun chips from granite—or the shine

on a river stone licked wet again like

sun catching the glasses set for lunch

on the tongue that touched my sun

burnt cheek, like my own flame sprung.

They Call Them Desire Lines

the shortcuts students wear in the grass
between concrete sidewalks on campus

or the diagonal trails that appear
in winter on the sides of ridges here,

paths cut by deer seeking water or food
in snow. My love packs, gasses up Fridays

to drive through driving rain behind semis
until he stops at the length of my body

like a truck that's lost its brakes and must
swerve onto a ramp of banked gravel.

He won't fly through red lights, honking, or
rear-end a sedan with kids strapped in back,

nor has he yet figured out how he will tow
his heavy machine out of so many stones.

Viking Ribstones, Alberta

We took grid-roads through towns with one church
past turn lanes for gas stations and grain elevators,

past fenced buffalo and flat, brown fields. Pavement
gave way to soil where the land lifts, turns to a knoll

I'll never find again on my own: that small gravel lot
near erratics sunk in grass, smooth as quartzite statues,

smooth as the palms and fingers that stroked and stroked
until they became a buffalo and her calf, asleep, ribs shining.

Long ago, people came to wait, pray, rub their hunger into
stones until herds appeared like dark clouds on the horizon.

From need, they made, and from gratitude. They still come,
leave tobacco, sweet grass, silver coins on the lawn mowed

around stone carcasses. They tie cloth strips onto twigs
just dazzling into leaf that morning we sat behind

the grove, looking over a plowed field's torn furrows
as the sun singed my shoulders' winter skin.

Amaryllis

He who plants the ear, shall he not hear?
Psalm 94:6

Who set the heart's bulb
in the chest, shall he not

bless the blade that tears
husk, parts earth, thrusts

a green budded shaft
to blast this scarlet horn

gaping, straining toward
a window's pane,

whoever lit this winter
sun, does he not love love?

Freshet

Born when the mountain rushes
with sudden, small streams,

when coltsfoot shoves its hooves—
thick-stemmed, fringed suns—

up through dead leaves,
and the sumac's maroon torches

 finally fade, Love, leave
your desk, come to the woods

where all is urge and bird-flurry
yearning toward sky.

Goats

My goats have almost never been broken
or duped into pulling a wagon. Not sheep,
my goats graze alone and could clear thistles
from your pasture. My goats climb up a cliff
and nibble. My goat carried your shame
into the wilderness, then shook it off.
A billy bends down and pees on his forelock
to lure the nanny. *Women are all goat
below the neck*, a pig said, but these goats
are all in my head. They rollick at night,
more I think, the worse it gets. Tied to tracks,
my goat vomits and flags the train. *Eat me
when I'm fatter*, my goats taunt the troll.
These goats are hard on fences and hedgerows.

Helpmate

rebuilt and painted the root cellar door
so our vacant-faced neighbor who follows

her husband of fifty years won't trip
into a cement crypt. *I am her protector,*

he says as she shuffles behind him, mutter-
ing in the alley. He shovels gravel into the ruts

last night's rainstorm cut like sorrow,
which just comes without courting it.

Yet here's a smooth silence where
the storm door used to screech. Listen:

I can open and close it while we talk
on the phone, only now you don't know

that I've slipped onto the back stoop
to stretch out under the million

heart-shaped leaves of the old catalpa tree.
Once trouble's courtesan, struggle's

true love, I now come home to a quiet
kitchen, your cup and bowl on the drainer;

the repaired faucet pull smoothly glides
on and off, cold and hot.

October Snow

All afternoon it fell
onto leaves until branches
bent with moans or wails
or broke with gunshots.

Snow clotted the lawn
I'd meant to mow that day,
so, I beat the lilac bush
with a straw broom

but still couldn't keep
dogwood limbs, draped
with bloody leaves,
from coming down,

then power lines, then
the house grew cold.
Ice cream softened
in its box as the town

succumbed, silent
except for the low hum
of trailer trucks hauling
freight out on route 80,

and of the generators
that sustain our elders
in their shared rooms
at the public home.

Luck

Across a parking lot, through automatic doors
where decades before they wheeled me out

with an infant on my lap, then strapped the baby
in back, *Good luck!* but this time, I wore a mask,

paused so a receptionist could scan my forehead,
offered my name, his name and room number, took

an elevator with other silent masks to his floor,
where nurses wore glittery clogs and bright scrubs,

thin gestures of cheer. When I reached the room
he shared with an old man so undone by pain

and hospital food, he refused to eat anything
but ice cream, I heard a heart like my baby's heart

long ago, and paused at the door where a machine
hid his bed, fan splayed across a wide screen

like the sonogram of a fetus, streaked with stars
arching through static: not a baby but a sea creature

shifting in the current, opening and closing,
determined to beat—not like a drum or a gong,

not like a clock, not even to pump like an engine,
but to surge—not with blood, but with light,

that held me awhile at that threshold.

Home Farm

The year I moved back to where I was born,
one clear afternoon driving up Route 655 toward
Great Aunt Twila at the rest home, a detour turned me

toward Jack's Mountain. To get back to my road
I veered again, circled in on the home from behind,
and there, across the road: thick smoke, fire trucks,

hoses on the berm at my uncle's farm—no, the cousins
have it now, Keith and Kent—where some summer
afternoons as a kid I pushed a feed cart: *shush, shush,*

surge of electric milkers, a wood-handled scoop
trailed feed under the Holsteins' slimy noses, spring
whisk mixed the formula for calves that sucked

from a rubber-nippled bucket, then sucked my thumb
with raspy tongues. Paste-eyed kittens lapped milk
from a basin set on sparkling barn snow in the center

of the cleanest stable in Mifflin county. *Wish, wish* pumped
the fly spray's wand. Cousins in home-sewn skirts won
4H ribbons for blue-blooded heifers. We climbed bales

in the fragrant haymow. Sun slanted through dust
in the granary like oil light in Dutch master paintings.
I remember when the barn burned in '47, Twila said,

full of hay, flames so high folks watched it blaze all night,
up and down the Valley. What happened then: electric spark
at milking time and grandpa, my teenaged Dad and uncle Dave

dragged out half the bawling herd before the joists come down.
Barn lost, reeking of burnt beef, firemen doused the house.
All winter men dragged logs from the mountain to rebuild.

In the new millennium, barns are steel; the milking parlor,
a sunken pit like the place you get your oil changed, milk house
an office for the farmer's desk and computer. And cows,

their tails lopped off like boxers, lounge on cement, eat,
chew, lactate, then, roused by gentle Spanish-speaking men,
stroll to the milkers. Their hooves never touch grass.

Professors calibrate their feed; to raise enough corn and beans
Keith and Kent rent fields our grandpa once tenant-farmed.
Land-o-Lakes takes seventeen tons of milk a day, the manure

from 600 slides into a covered pit, warm as a cow's gut,
where it digests with plate scraps hauled in from restaurants
to make methane, to generate electricity to run the place

and a few more, leftovers sold back to the grid. Liquid
waste fertilizes the crops, and solids get dried for bedding.
When production goes up, power goes down, Keith laughs,

we teeter between milk and manure. Barn fire and a plan
hatched by brains in Berkley transformed this old farm
into a place I can't understand, so I spin myths of thwarted

intentions, past disasters in which it all turns out fine,
while upstate or west of here—places where milk checks
couldn't cover hybrid seeds, diesel, fertilizer, pesticide—

in fallow fields and dim hemlock forests, diamond-studded
drill bits bore through the earth and split black shale
with grit and chemicals to flush out precious what?

Methane, which these lazy cows just make without
much thought, the same way they make milk.

August Friday, Adirondacks

All afternoon I've watched hummingbirds needle
lemon lilies outside the cottage window, then
dart off, blossoms bobbing on their stalks.

All day pontoon planes have whined like wasps
in the distance. Wives and children wait on docks
in these lakes for men to emerge in city suits.

This time of year, sun glazes water with a clarity
I've come to associate with the end of romance
or vacation. Meteors streak the sky. Sometimes

when I wonder what will finally come of this
life, I think of the one professor who ever
listened to me. Where might he be tonight?

Brooklyn, sipping wine in a garden: one wife,
no children, some slender books, a brownstone
that won't stay restored—all he can show

for his work. Each year, students come from farther
away, he said, then graduate without a backward glance
or trace of the talk that sparked between them.

Gulls

startle these streets where I'm never quite at ease,
shriek from terracotta rooftop pipes, smash

whatever peace I breathed from heaping pots of pink
and purple petunias hung down along the Liffy.

Fox kits haunt a construction site at Trinity
where I watched a gull pierce a boxed sandwich

with his beak, shred plastic, extract strips of cheese
while magpies and smaller gulls looked on, overlord

who defends and eats his hoard at once. *Free lunch!*
I nodded to a man in worker's pants. *Always*

a free lunch for that fella. He's a regular!
Our high-ceilinged Georgian rooms, crowned

with egg and dart molding so clotted with paint
the darts seem plump enough to bloom.

We feast at a cafe table outside Dublin Castle,
but *Look!* that other plate heaped with mussels.

Mostly shell and air, comparison, thief of bliss.
Another shrill angel interrupts, shrapnel blast

from a civil war that burned parchments
at the National Archives into charred cabbages.

Yes, but isn't spectacle what we want? What
we want, at our age, may be just to know

what we want—*stir with a knife, trouble and strife*—
and to live content with what we get.

Outer Banks Epithalamium

Who can resist the rhythmic rumble
that first soothed us in the womb,
tides of endless approach and retreat,
smooth slide of foam over bare toes,
and the release of small, tumbled gifts?

Why not meet where creatures first
crawled from the depths to breathe, where
slaves stepped into waves and walked out
of Egypt, where Jesus climbed from a boat
and told the furious storm to rest?

Walking the beach, who does not pause
to gaze out beyond the breakers to that line
where sea and sky meet, and to launch
whatever sorrows they've brought
to that place? If you choose to wade

beyond the crashing, let your body
lift from the sand, weightless. If the rip
tide pulls you out, don't resist, swim
across the current then back to shore.
Call or wave. Never go out alone.

Meditation at Panama City Beach, Florida

the careless corrupt state is all black specks
too far apart, and ugly whites
—Elizabeth Bishop, "Florida"

Each day for six weeks I walk a wide, white beach among white-
       haired white people, mostly, in a place where Spain found
it strategic to welcome those escaped from slavery
       in the colony named for King George—if they'd convert
or enlist—and I think of growing up with a postal address of Irwin, PA,

       sundown town in a coalfield, with a better library
and schools than we endured out on rural delivery route 6,
       plus Saturday matinees. During cartoons and trailers, we ran
the aisles; once I climbed onto a stage probably built for minstrels
       and wound myself up in that ancient red drape stinking

of popcorn butter, sticky floor. What comes of not seeing
       where you are? Lately, my father said when the Hill burned
in Pittsburgh after Dr. King's murder, someone lit a cross
       on a hill by the old Lutheran church at Brush Creek. Brush
Creek Elementary, my four-room brick school built in 1901,

       no black or brown children. When a flashlight bobbed
between cinema seats to search our white faces,
       I was back in my place, blameless. Years later, I read
onstage with Yusef Komunyakaa at VMI, afterward two cadets
       in grey uniforms escorted us downtown. We left the boys

at the bar, but when I begged to cut through the cemetery
        where Lee and his war horse lay buried, Yusef refused.
Softly. Firmly, until I made him explain *I am a Black man.*
        You are a white woman. This is the South after dark.
I fell dumb as Teddy Roosevelt who'd invited Booker T. Washington

        to dine at the White House with the President's wife
and daughter, prompting a senator from Carolina to say,
        Now we shall have to kill a thousand n------
to get them back in their places. A White House spokesman
        denied that the first lady and daughter were there.

Sun blazes off the sand, quartz fine as salt washed down
        from the weary Appalachians which once loomed as high
as the Himalayas. In Irwin, just sixty years after Roosevelt
        confessed that his white wife and daughter had, indeed,
dined with the Black professor, my parents told us to put on our PJs

        and drove us to see *Guess Who's Coming to Dinner.*
We fell asleep in the back seat, but not before *the glory*
        of love touched down on the other coast, where later
a jury acquitted OJ, and cheers burst from New York City's streets
        and from the secretary seated outside my professor's office.

He stuck his head out to ask what on earth—on her desk radio
        and Walkmans on Washington Place—had just occurred. Pelicans
and war planes troll the panhandle some still call *Redneck Riviera,*
        Panama City, named for an isthmus Roosevelt acquired in 1903,
Bay County seat, where the sheriff transported Claude Neal

        to save him from a gathering mob, then sailed him out
the coast, jail to jail, all the way to Alabama. Six men followed, broke
        into the jail, kidnapped Neal, and drove him back home
to torture and kill (look it up, if you will), claiming he'd strangled
        Lola Cannady, a white woman. Two thousand gathered

to destroy his corpse, which a sheriff hung from a live oak that still
        grows, swathed in gray moss, beside a new courthouse
in Mariana, an hour's drive north of this pristine beach.
        That was 1934, one year before my father was born
up in the Ridge and Valley. Now young people want to cut

        down the tree, according to WFSU; elders wish to erect
a marker and preserve it. *This was the last place he was*
        on earth, said Neal's nephew. Neal's kin changed
the name to Smith, yet some still walk around there *like zombies.*
        If Neal and Cannady had been lovers, the white men

would also have killed him. All of our bodies: fish, amphibian,
        reptile, bird, and mammal, wrote Rachel Carson, who grew up
north of Pittsburgh along the Allegheny, carry in our veins a stream
        of sodium, potassium, and calcium in almost the same
proportions as the water of the sea. In 1941, Panama City's mayor lifted

        the first shovel of sand to make Tyndall Air Force Base, dug
into *stubborn palmettos*, Wikipedia says, no mention of the displaced—
        boat builders and fishermen, sportsmen's guides for northerners,
the church and school at Redfish Point since long before statehood—
        descended from Seminoles, Africans, Spanish stowaways.

Each crystal of sand washed into creeks, carried into the sea,
        displaces precisely the same amount of water, Carson wrote.
I grow weary of beauty. As long as people won't agree
        about what to do with the old live oak growing
up in Mariana, the county commissioners get to do nothing.

Unnamed Tributary

Name it sun splashing on wet rock.

Call it adelgid-brittle twig of hemlock,

shale outcrop of the Appalachian

Revolution. Call it stone bed, stone wall,

not far from man-made foundations,

not far from an ancient apple tree.

Call it fern preserve, root splay,

all manner of moss. Call it crayfish

where the stream deepens and bends.

Say iridescence of damsel fly,

wing black night far from cities.

Name it refuge, regeneration,

safehold, shadow home.

NOTES

"Testing"—"Let not your hearts be troubled" begins John 14, wherein Jesus anticipates his death. "Woman behold your son . . ." quotes John 19 where, from the cross, Jesus instructs his mother to take for her son the disciple, and for John to make Mary his mother, modeling a form of community not dependent on kinship. "No harm will befall you . . ." (Psalm 91) quotes prayers provided in Hebrew and English on a telephone hotline for those dying from Covid-19, "Ultraorthodox Jewish Traditions Upended by Coronovirus," *New York Times*, April 16, 2020. "Hope is a thing with feathers," is the first line of Emily Dickinson's poem 314. The sentence attributed to Thomas Merton can be found in *The Monastic Journey*.

"Gideons"—The story of the ancient Hebrew prophet Gideon can be found in Judges 6–8. The line attributed to Mussolini is paraphrased from "Mussolini Declares Liberty Is Outworn," *New York Times*, March 30, 1923. The words of Mariann E. Budde, Episcopal bishop of Washington, appeared in a story about the Black Lives Matter movement, "Protesters Dispersed with Tear Gas so Trump Could Pose at Church," *New York Times*, June 1, 2020.

"American Chestnut Plantation"—The first quotation alludes to "The Village Blacksmith," a nineteenth-century ballad by Henry Wadsworth Longfellow as well as the site of the lovers' betrayal in George Orwell's *1984*. The second quoted line is drawn from "The Christmas Song" by Robert Wells and Mel Tormé, popularlized by Nat King Cole. The final quotes are idiomatic expressions that gesture toward rescue and repetitive stories or tropes.

"As Is" repeatedly alludes to Erika Meitner's collection of poems *Holy Moly Carry Me* and is dedicated to her. The words attributed to Stalin were reported in an article by Leonard Lyons in the *Washington Post,* January 30, 1947.

The "When I Say . . ." poems follow a pattern devised by Geffrey Davis for a series titled "What I Mean When I Say . . ." gathered in his first collection *Revising the Storm.*

"Waking Up with Jerry Sandusky" refers to the former football coach and convicted sex offender who gained access to children through his affiliation with Penn State.

"*Bruder*" remembers Mervin E. Horst, 1961–2022.

"Gulls" is for Helen O'Leary.

"August Friday, Adirondacks" remembers Gordon Pardl, 1944–2020.

"Outer Banks Epithalamium" celebrates the 2019 marriage of Jo Lena Fullwood and Laura Brenneman.

"Meditation at Panama City Beach" cites information about "the last spectacular lynching" in the United States in "'Haven't Quite Shaken the Horror': Howard Kester, the Lynching of Claude Neal, and Social Activism in the South during the 1930s," by Joshua Youngblood in *Florida Historical*

Quarterly, summer 2007, and "Revisiting Claude Neal Lynching Brings Opportunity For Racial Healing In Jackson County," August 24, 2020, news.wfsu.org. The Rachel Carson references, including the final image in the poem, come from *The Sea Around Us.*

"Unnamed Tributary" is a phrase that commonly marks the location of small streams on maps, and "safehold" in the final line alludes to the title of a collection of poems by Ann Hostetler.

ACKNOWLEDGMENTS

I am grateful to the following journals and their editors for first publishing a number of these poems, sometimes in slightly different forms: *Antioch Review, Centered, Chautauqua, Christian Century, Ekstasis, Epoch, GUEST: A Journal of Guest Editors,* Melanie Dennis Unrau, ed., *The Mennonite, Poetry in a Time of Pandemic, On the Seawall,* and *Reformed Journal.*

"War" was published as "The Visiting Poet" in *The Fourth River.*

"American Bittersweet," "Home Farm," and "They Call it a Strip Job," appeared in *Mountains Piled Upon Mountains: Appalachian Nature Writing in the Anthropocene* (WVU Press, 2019), edited by Jessica Cory.

"American Chestnut Plantation," "Dialogue with Lake Perez," "Eastern Box Turtle," "Lake Trail, January," "Unnamed Tributary" and "What the Hemlock Said" belong to the Long-Term Ecological Reflections Project (*Creek Journals*) founded by Ian Marshall at Shaver's Creek Environmental Center in Petersburg, Pennsylvania.

Thanks to Penn State's Department of English in the College of Liberal Arts and to Mark Morrison, head of Penn State's the Humanities Institute, for leaves during which some of these poems were written.

Special thanks to Izzy whose unfortunate quarantine during study abroad gave me a week to focus on the manuscript when I needed it most.

Many other students, colleagues, and friends have lifted my spirits and inspired me in ways too numerous to name or even recall, but I will thank Christopher

Campbell, Robert Caserio, Cecil Giscombe, Pearl Gluck, Ann Hostetler, Alison Jaenecke, Elizabeth Kadetsky, Nancy Locke, Chris Reed, Steven Rubin, Danielle Ryle, Sheila Squilliante, Lisa Sternlieb, Mary Vollero, Ruby Wiebe, and Susan Wheeler, longtime friend and brilliant reader of some of these poems. In addition, Kimberly Q. Andrews, Nicole Cooley, Jeff Gundy, Shara McCallum, Abby Minor, and Sofia Samatar read the entire collection at various stages and offered comments and responses that made it stronger.

Thank you, Helen O'Leary, for the perfect cover image and many cups of tea.

I also thank Terrance Hayes, Nancy Krygowski, and Jeffrey McDaniel for choosing to publish this book, especially Nancy, for her kindness and insight throughout the process.

To everyone at the University of Pittsburgh Press, including Ed Ochester and Alex Wolfe, my deep gratitude for a long affiliation and for your care with this new collection.

Mom and Dad who, with my brothers and their wives, drew closer in our collective frailty these past years, and Phil and Amelia, my constants: your significance far exceeds whatever forms it may find in poems.